First World War
and Army of Occupation
War Diary
France, Belgium and Germany

57 DIVISION
172 Infantry Brigade
King's (Liverpool Regiment)
2/9 Battalion
6 September 1915 - 24 February 1916

WO95/2985/3

The Naval & Military Press Ltd
www.nmarchive.com
Published in association with The National Archives

Published by

The Naval & Military Press Ltd

Unit 10 Ridgewood Industrial Park,

Uckfield, East Sussex,

TN22 5QE England

Tel: +44 (0) 1825 749494

www.naval-military-press.com

www.nmarchive.com

This diary has been reprinted in facsimile from the original. Any imperfections are inevitably reproduced and the quality may fall short of modern type and cartographic standards.

© **Crown Copyright**
Images reproduced by permission of The National Archives, London, England, 2015.

Contents

Document type	Place/Title	Date From	Date To
Heading	WO95/2985/3 57 Divn. 172 Inf Brig 2/9 King's Liverpool Regt 1915 Sept-1916 Feb		
Heading	War Diary And Intelligence Summary 2/9th Battalion "The King's" (Liverpool Regiment) T.F. Period from 1st September, 1915 to 30th Septr. 1915		
War Diary	Oxted	06/09/1915	30/09/1915
Heading	2/9th Battalion "The King's" Liverpool Regiment War Diary From October 1st 1915 To October 31st 1915		
War Diary	Tandridge Camp Oxted	02/10/1915	30/10/1915
Heading	War Diary And Summary Of Events And Information Headquarters 2/9th Bn. King's Liverpool Regiment Period November 1st 1915 To November 30th 1915		
War Diary	Maidstone Kent	01/11/1915	30/11/1915
Heading	War Diary Of Headquarters 2/9th Battalion The King's (Liverpool Regiment) December 1st 1915 To December 31st 1915		
War Diary	Maidstone	13/12/1915	30/12/1915
Heading	War Diary January 1916		
War Diary	Maidstone	05/01/1916	31/01/1916
Heading	War Diary Of 2/9th Battalion The King's (Liverpool Regiment) Period 1st February 1916 To 29th February 1916		
War Diary	Maidstone	24/02/1916	24/02/1916

WO 95 2985/3

57 Divn. 172 Inf Brig
2/9 King's Liverpool Regt
1915 Sept - 1916 Feb

WAR DIARY AND

INTELLIGENCE SUMMARY.

2/9th Battalion " THE KING'S" (Liverpool Regiment).T.F.

Period from 1st September, 1915 to 30 h Septr.1915.

Army Form C. 2118.

2/9th Battn. "KING'S" (L'pool Regt).T.F. **WAR DIARY** or **INTELLIGENCE SUMMARY.**

TANDRIDGE CAMP, OXTED. October 3rd 1915

(Erase heading not required.)

Instructions regarding War Diaries and Intelligence Summaries are contained in F.S. Regs., Part II and the Staff Manual respectively. Title pages will be prepared in manuscript.

Hour, Date, Place	Summary of Events and Information	Remarks and references to Appendices
OXTED.		
4.0.p.m. 6.9.1915.	Colonel R. Eccles granted sick furlough to 5th October, 1915.	
3.0.p.m. 11.9.1915.	2/Lieut. A. G. Warde joined for duty from 44th Provl.Battn.T.F.	
9.0.a.m. 13.9.1915.	2/Lieut. E. Gardiner to II Army School of Signalling, TUNBRIDGE WELLS.	
9.0.a.m. 13.9.1915.	2/Lieut. G. F. Buckle, 2/Lieut. A. E. Hunt, 2/Lieut. W. Abbott to O.T.C. Emmanuel College, CAMBRIDGE.	
11.0.a.m. 18.9.1915.	2/Lieut. F. T. Easby left this station to rejoin 16th Service Battn. "KING'S" (Liverpool Regiment) Prees Heath, WHITCHURCH, SALOP.	
18.9.1915.	Lieut. H. H. Wilkinson rejoined for duty as A/Adjutant, from Course at CHELSEA.	
8.0.a.m. 21.9.1915.	Corpl. O'Byrne to Pioneer Course at WROTHAM (COMMENCING 22nd.)	
12.0.noon 21.9.1915.	3120 Pte. J. Robb to AYLESFORD Vet.Hospital for Cold Shoeing Course.	
12.30.noon 30th.9.1915.	Lieut. P. Diggery and Lieut. E. Payne left this station to proceed to SOUTHAMPTON for duty with the linked 1st Line Unit, Overseas.	

Comand.g. 2/9th Battalion "THE KING'S" (Liverpool Regiment). T.F.

.... Major.
T.F.

2/9th. Battalion "The King's" Liverpool Regiment.

WAR   DIARY

from October 1st. 1915

to October 31st. 1915.

WAR DIARY or INTELLIGENCE SUMMARY.

2/9th Battalion "THE KING'S" (Liverpool Regt.) T.F.

Army Form C. 2118.

MAIDSTONE. KENT. November 3rd 1915.

(Erase heading not required.)

Instructions regarding War Diaries and Intelligence Summaries are contained in F.S. Regs., Part II. and the Staff Manual respectively. Title pages will be prepared in manuscript.

Hour, Date, Place	Summary of Events and Information	Remarks and references to Appendices
TANDRIDGE CAMP, OXTED.		
2. 10. 15.	2/Lieut. E. Gardiner returned from Signalling Course at TUNBRIDGE WELLS.	
4. 10. 15. 9.0.a.m.	2/Lieut. A. Berry to Course of Instruction at BLACKHEATH.	
4. 10. 15. 8.0.p.m.	2/Lieut. R. E. Ewans joined for duty.	
4. 10. 15. 9.0.a.m.	2933 Sergt. J. H. Jackson to Musketry Course, BISLEY.	
6. 10. 15. 6.45.a.m.	Brigade Course in Bayonet Fighting - 12 N.C.O's attended.	
6. 10. 15. 12.0.noon	2/Lieuts. G. E. Morton and W. H. Challiner to SOUTHAMPTON for 1/9th Bn. Overseas.	
7. 10. 15. 8.30.a.m.	Two men attended Cold Shoeing examination at Hqrs. 57th (W.L.) Div. Train.	
11.10.15. 9.0.a.m.	No. 3534 Corpl. J. McEwan to Machine Gun Course at BISLEY.	
11.10. 15.	2/Lieuts. W. Abbott, G.F. Buckle & A.E. Hunt returned from Course at CAMBRIDGE.	
11.10. 15.	Local Musketry Course - 6 Officers & 10 N.C.O's attended.	
12.10. 15. 9.0.a.m.	2912 Sergt. T. Roberts to Grenadier Course at GODSTONE.	
14.10. 15. 2.0.p.m.	2/Lieut. L.H. Cockram, No.2645 Sergt. J. Brown & Officers servant to WROTHAM - Pioneer Course.	
15.10. 15.	Five N.C.O's attended Local Course in Bayonet Fighting.	
16.10. 15. 8.0.p.m.	2/Lieut. A. Berry finished Local Course at BLACKHEATH.	
16.10.15. 11.15.a.m.	2/Lieut. W. Monks joined for duty.	
17.10. 15. 4.0.p.m.	BRIGADE TEST FIRE ALARM.	
19.10. 15. 9.0.a.m.	2/Lieut. B. Osborne joined for duty as Transport Officer.	
19.10. 15. 9.0.a.m.	2/Lieut. W. Monks to CAMBRIDGE UNIVERSITY O.T.C. } Elementary Course.	
20.10. 15. 8.0.a.m.	2/Lieut. H. J. Hallett to Grenadier Course at WROTHAM.	
21.10. 15. 8.0.a.m.	2/Lieut. R. D. Grossart & 4 N.C.O's to MAIDSTONE on Billeting duty.	
22.10. 15. 8.15.a.m.	2/Lieut. W. Abbott & 6 Other ranks to MAIDSTONE as cleaning party.	
23.10. 15. 5.0.a.m.	Battalion left for WILDERNESSE, SEAL. Arriving 1.50.p.m.	
23.10. 15. 7.55.a.m.	BRIGADE ALARM at SEAL.	
26.10. 15. 3.55.p.m.	Battalion left SEAL for MAIDSTONE. ARRIVED MAIDSTONE at 2.30.p.m.	
29.10. 15.	BATTALION ALARM.	
30.10. 15.	2/Lieut. H. J. Hallett returned from Course at WROTHAM.	
	Colonel Robert Eccles died.	

Commanding 2/9th Battalion "THE KING'S" (Liverpool Regiment). T.F.

Major.

WAR DIARY

AND

SUMMARY OF EVENTS AND INFORMATION

Headquarters
2/9th.Bn.King's Liverpool Regiment.

PERIOD

November 1st 1915
to
November 30th.1915

Stone street
Maidstone
December 4th.1915.

Army Form C. 2118.

WAR DIARY
or
INTELLIGENCE SUMMARY.   2/9th Battn. "KING'S" (Lpool Regt.) T.F.

(Erase heading not required.)

Instructions regarding War Diaries and Intelligence Summaries are contained in F.S. Regs., Part II and the Staff Manual respectively. Title pages will be prepared in manuscript.

HEADQUARTERS December 3rd, 1915.

DATE 3/12/15
No. 2274 A

Place	Hour, Date	Summary of Events and Information	Remarks and references to Appendices
MAIDSTONE. KENT.			
	November 1st, 9.0.a.m.	2/Lieut. A. G. Potter to BISLEY on Machine Gun Course.	
	November 1st, 2.0.p.m.	No.2912 Sergt. D. Kelly to WROTHAM, II Army School of Trench Warfare.	
	November 3rd, 9.0.a.m.	No.1942 Corpl. W. Heap to Course in Vet. First Aid at AYLESFORD.	
	November 3rd, 10.0.a.m.	No.2249 Sergt. A. Kelly to Grenadier Course at GODSTONE.	
	November 5th, 5.0.p.m.	2/Lieut. L. H. Cockran reported from Course at WROTHAM.	
	November 8th, 2.0.p.m.	No. 3265 Lance Corpl. Winstanley to AYLESFORD Course of Instruction	
	November 9th, 3.0.p.m.	2/Lieut. A. E. Hunt to Pioneer Course, WROTHAM.	
	November 10th, 9.0.a.m.	Six N.C.O's attended Brigade Class in Physical Training.	
	November 11th, 1.17.p.m.	2/Lieut. L. H. Cockran proceeded to SOUTHAMPTON for overseas	
	November 15th, 2.0.p.m.	2/Lieut. G. F. Buckle and No.3525 Corpl. S. Bromilow to II Army School of Trench Warfare at WROTHAM.	
	November 15th, 9.0.a.m.	No.2852 Serg. O'Byrne to Rifle Course at BISLEY.	
	November 15th, 10.0.a.m.	3005 L/Cpl. R.C. Jones & 3757 L/Cpl. J. Lacey to Cookery Course at ORCHARD HOSPITAL? DARTFORD.	
	November 15th, 6.0.p.m.	2/Lieut. W. Monks returned from Course at CAMBRIDGE O.T.C.	
	November 17th, 9.0.a.m.	2/Lieuts. R. E. Evans and A. Berry to General Course at OXFORD. O.T.C.	
	November 23rd.	Inspection by G.O.C. 172nd Infantry Brigade.	
	November 26th, 11.30.am.	Inspection by Major E.T. Dickson, Inspector of Territorial Infantry.	
	November 27th, 10.40.am.	BATTALION ALARM	
	November 30th, 9.42.am.	BRIGADE ALARM	
	November 30th.	2/Lieut. A. E. Hurt returned from Course at WROTHAM,	

.... Major.
Commanding 2/ 9th Battalion "THE KING'S" (Liverpool Regiment).T.F.

WAR DIARY

of

HEADQUARTERS

2/9TH BATTALION THE KING'S (LIVERPOOL REGIMENT)

December 1st 1915

to

December 31st 1915.

MAIDSTONE

5th January 1916.

Army Form C. 2118.

WAR DIARY
or
INTELLIGENCE SUMMARY.
(Erase heading not required.)

17th Batt Liverpool Regiment

Hour, Date, Place	Summary of Events and Information	Remarks and references to Appendices
MAIDSTONE		
13th December 1915	The Battalion was inspected at Company Training by the G.O.C. 172nd Infantry Brigade	D.F.
20th "	The G.O.C. 57th West Lancashire Division inspected the Battalion on an outpost scheme	D.F.
20th "	Fifty eight (58) Other Ranks medically unfit for General Service proceeded to Ramsgate on transfer to 44th Provisional Battn	D.F.
21st "	The G.O.C. II Army Central Force inspected the Battalion	D.F.
30th "	The Commandant of the School of Musketry HYTHE inspected the Battalion at Musketry	D.F.

D.F. Dean Myers
Commdg 17th Liverpool Regiment

2/9th BN. "THE KING'S" (L'POOL RGT.) T.F.

HEADQUARTERS
DATE 3-2-16
No. 429
2/9th BN. "THE KING'S"
(L'POOL REGT.) T.F.

War Diary,

January 1916.

January 1916

Army Form C. 2118.

2/9th Bn. "THE KING'S" (L'POOL REGT.) I.F.

WAR DIARY
or
INTELLIGENCE SUMMARY.
(Erase heading not required.)

Instructions regarding War Diaries and Intelligence Summaries are contained in F.S. Regs., Part II and the Staff Manual respectively. Title pages will be prepared in manuscript.

Hour, Date, Place	Summary of Events and Information	Remarks and references to Appendices
January 5th 1916 Maidotte	Twenty five Home Service details proceeded to join the 4th Provision at Battalion at Ramsgate.	T.A.
" 8th "	Lieut Col J.J. Parkinson T.D. resumed command of the 2/9th Batt'n Liverpool Regiment	T.A.
" 11th "	The G.O.C. 57th West Lancashire Division inspected the Battalion at Files bank.	T.A.
22nd – 31st.	During this period 65 recruits to take under the Group System joined the Battalion from the Administrative Centre 9th Batt'n Liverpool Regiment. Liverpool.	T.A.

J.J. Parkinson, Lieut Colonel
Commdg 2/9th Batt'n Liverpool Regiment

WAR DIARY

of

X(th 2/9TH BATTALION THE KING'S (LIVERPOOL
REGIMENT).

Period
1st February 1916 to 29th February 1916

Maidstone
8th March 1916

February 1916

WAR DIARY
2/9th Bn. THE KING'S (L'POOL REGT) T.F.
or
INTELLIGENCE SUMMARY
(Erase heading not required.)

Army Form C. 2118.

Hour, Date, Place	Summary of Events and Information	Remarks and references to Appendices
24th February 1916 Maidstone	The Battalion was warned to hold itself in readiness to move in the event of an alarm.	M.S.
February 1916 Maidstone	Sixty one (61) Grouped Recruits received from the Admin: details Centre 9th Br. Liverpool Regiment during the month.	M.S.

M.S. Anderson
Lieut Colonel
Commanding 2/9th Bn Liverpool Regiment